IMAGES
of America

AMHERST AND HADLEY
MASSACHUSETTS

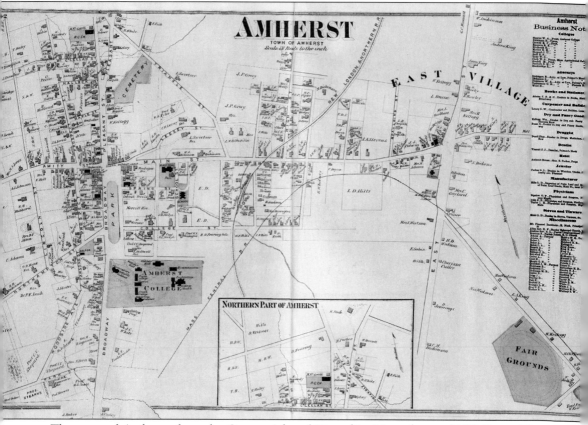

The town of Amherst, from the *County Atlas of Hampshire Massachusetts* (F.W. Beers, New York, 1873).

IMAGES
of America

AMHERST AND HADLEY
MASSACHUSETTS

Daniel Lombardo

ARCADIA

First published 1997
Copyright © Daniel Lombardo, 1997

ISBN 0-7524-0483-0

Published by Arcadia Publishing,
an imprint of the Chalford Publishing Corporation
One Washington Center, Dover, New Hampshire 03820
Printed in Great Britain

Library of Congress Cataloging-in-Publication Data applied for

Contents

Acknowledgments

All photographs courtesy of the Jones Library, Inc., Amherst, Massachusetts.
Thanks to the Johnson family, who donated the Clifton Johnson Photograph Collection
to the Jones Library (many of the photographs in the Hadley sections are by Clifton Johnson).
Thanks to Dorothy Russell and the Hadley Historical Society,
to Jamie Carter and Arcadia Publishing,
and special thanks to Karen Banta.

Daniel Lombardo
292 Main Rd.
Westhampton, MA 01027

Introduction

Amherst and Hadley are ghost towns. On the surface Hadley suffers from the pace of twentieth-century life, but just off the main road the Hadley Common looks much as it always has. A broad green with the Connecticut River curving at one end, its eighteenth and nineteenth-century homes conjure up the Porter and Hopkins families and the old Bull's Head Tavern.

Amherst, once a part of Hadley, went off on its own and now attracts international attention. The town seethes with the cultural excitement of its three institutions of higher learning—Amherst College, Hampshire College, and the University of Massachusetts. Walk down Main Street, however, and the air becomes hushed as you approach the brick Dickinson Homestead. Emily Dickinson still seems to inhabit her small second-floor room. There are flowers in the garden, and the path Emily used to walk can still be seen leading to her brother Austin's house.

Austin and Susan Dickinson's place, known as the Evergreens, stands next door, looking much as it did the day Austin's coffin was carried out in 1895. Both houses are surrounded by ancient trees, and one expects to see a carriage with a span of bay horses pull out carrying the Dickinsons—all but Emily—to the Congregational church before riding out to the Pelham Hills. The stone church the Dickinsons helped build stands as it did the night Emily saw it for the first time in the moonlight. And the Dickinson Homestead looks out, as Emily did, to the Pelham Hills.

In 1659, Reverend John Russell led his dissenting Congregationalists from Wethersfield and Hartford, Connecticut, to the place they would call Hadley. By 1728 the settlers had begun to spread to the part of town then known as the Third Precinct. In 1759 Hadley granted the families in the East Precinct the right to govern themselves as a separate district. The name Amherst was given by Governor Pownell in honor of General Jeffery Amherst, the somewhat notorious commander and hero of the English armies in the colonies.

Pugnacious Amherst has always thought for itself. The town was not initially enthusiastic about the Revolution when Sam Adams sent for support in 1772. Then, after having joined the Revolution and helping win independence, many in town rebelled against the new government by taking part in Shays Rebellion in 1786. Amherst was also against the War of 1812. At a town meeting co-chaired by Emily Dickinson's grandfather, a veiled threat was made to secede from the union. Today the Amherst Common, one of the prettiest in New England, is often a site where people express their local views to the world. And the world, not always sure what to make of the town, often listens.

The Amherst and Hadley area of the Connecticut River Valley has produced a most amazing variety of true geniuses—and true eccentrics. Washington Irving sensed something unusual there in 1832, when he wrote "I have had a most delightful excursion along the enchanting Valley of the Connecticut—of which I dare not speak at present—for it is just now the topic which I am a little mad upon. It is a perfect stream for a poet."

Irving had no way of knowing that Emily Dickinson was just then almost eighteen months old. She would make hardly a ripple in that poetic stream during her lifetime, but today is celebrated as one of the world's finest poets in the English language.

Like most New England towns, the Amherst area diversified in the nineteenth century. Particularly after the Civil War, the African-American and Irish populations increased. Many African-Americans worked in the homes of Amherst professors or did manual labor; some went into business and professional work. The Irish were hired to build the New London Northern Railroad, the Congregational church on Main Street, the Episcopal church on the Common, and the first buildings of the Agricultural College. On the surface there was harmony, even affection for some, like Henry Jackson and Charley Thompson, who were well-respected members of the black community. Underneath there was discrimination, however, and when a street fight broke out in 1885 between African-Americans and Irish, it was reported more as a sporting event than a symptom of social breakdown.

Though known for education as early as 1814, Amherst in the nineteenth century was nearly as well known for its palm leaf hat factories. By the 1890s the Hills and Burnett factories were shipping hundreds of thousands of hats across the country. Factory bells competed with college and church bells. Rivalries and feuds between factories added a new layer of competition to a town that loved to pit student teams or business teams against each other on the ball field or in the pool hall.

In 1897, for example, the Burnett Hat Factory raided a banquet put on by the Hills Factory. The Burnett people not only stole the ice cream for dessert, they took over the train the Hills people were to take to the banquet. A "stink pot" forced everyone outdoors. The next day their songs and noise irritated much of Amherst. Both factories went out of business in the mid-1930s, after tastes in hats changed.

The twentieth century brought major changes to the area. Just when local farming started to flag, Hadley agriculture was rejuvenated by Polish immigration. The small Massachusetts Agricultural College in Amherst became the University of Massachusetts. A new, highly innovative institution—Hampshire College—was opened in 1970. But concurrent with rapid growth was a determination to save the natural beauty of of the area by setting aside farmland, expanding conservation land, and restoring village landmarks.

Today, one can stand on the Amherst Common and feel the past, even as students throw frisbees or rush to classes. With the classic buildings of Amherst College at one end, and brick-front shops, churches, and the Lord Jeffery Amherst Inn surrounding it, the Common seems unbounded by time. At the Lord Jeff one imagines Robert Frost sitting on the veranda as he did during the years he taught and lived in Amherst. His voice can be heard reciting "Stopping by Woods on a Snowy Evening" as one contemplates his original manuscript at the Jones Library. Thoughts both large and small arise here as naturally as lines from Emily Dickinson. And it's no wonder that Frost himself contemplated the fate of the world and wrote his stunning poem "Fire and Ice" surrounded by the ghosts of Amherst and Hadley.

One
The Amherst Heart:
"Plain and Whole and Permanent and Warm"
—Emily Dickinson

A BIRD'S-EYE VIEW OF AMHERST, c. 1855. John Bachelder created the most detailed of the early prints of Amherst and published it in 1858. The First Congregational Church (left) was founded in 1739, when Amherst was known as the Third Precinct of Hadley. Reverend David Parson Jr.'s Tory sympathies caused a bitter rift, which led to the start of the Second Congregational Church in 1783. Town taxes continued to support the church for another fifty years, then ceased. By the 1850s, the Common was surrounded by Amherst College buildings on the south; a Baptist church, a hotel, shops, and small manufacturers on the west and north; and farms on the east.

A VIEW OF THE TOWN OF AMHERST, 1870s. Photographer John Lovell climbed the tower of Johnson Chapel at Amherst College to take this classic view of the town. Part swampy frog pond and part hayfield, the Common was also the parade ground for the local militia. In the nineteenth century, the Hampshire Agricultural Society held its fall cattle shows there. The Amherst Ornamental Tree Association, founded in 1857, took a more aesthetic view. In consultation with Frederick Law Olmsted, the association transformed the Common into a park-like setting in 1874.

LORD JEFFERY AMHERST. One of the many local ironies is the fact that Jeffery Amherst never set foot in the town that bears his name. In fact, Amherst wasn't the townspeople's choice. Lord Jeffery Amherst (1717–1797) was the British general who conquered and annexed Canada as the commander-in-chief of British forces. His capture of Louisbourg, Nova Scotia, in 1758, was his first great conquest. When, in 1759, the East Precinct of Hadley petitioned to separate from the town, Massachusetts Governor Pownell gave the new district the name of Amherst. Jeffery Amherst's mixed career also included the notorious gift of smallpox-infested blankets to the Pontiac Indians—an early example of biochemical warfare.

Main Street, Looking toward Pelham, *c.* 1840. One of the earliest images of Main Street, this J.C. Sharpe lithograph was used by David Mack Jr. & Son on their letterhead. The Macks produced hats at their straw works. The house where both the Macks and Emily Dickinson's family lived can be seen in the distance, on the left side of Main Street.

Main Street, Looking toward Pelham, 1856–1867. John Lovell took this rare photograph within a few years of becoming Amherst's first significant photographer in 1856. The view is similar to J.C. Sharpe's 1840 lithograph. Today's town hall is on the site of the "Brick Store" building on the right.

PHOENIX HALL, CORNER OF MAIN AND NORTH PEASANT STREETS, 1873. Named because it "rose out of the ashes" of a fire of the previous building in 1838, this marks the least changed of the four corners of Amherst center. For well over a century druggists like George Ellsbree and Henry Adams held this corner. R.W. Stratton sold boots and shoes next door, and Saxton and Burnell advertised as "First class watchmakers, fine jewelers, artistic engravers, skillful opticians." Cobbler William Newell lived and eked out a living on the second floor. In 1878 he was found dead there of malnutrition and pneumonia.

PHOENIX HALL, 1881. After innumerable fires, the town brought in running water on May 1, 1880, thus helping the legendary Phoenix Hall remain standing after this 1881 fire. Previously, Amherst firefighting was ineffectual, and entire blocks sometimes burned to the ground.

COOK'S BLOCK, 1881. The burned out upper floor of Phoenix Hall was redesigned, and the building was re-christened Cook's Block in 1881. Despite still more fires, it remains essentially intact today. Many businesses thrived here, including Charles King's barber shop. In 1885, however, King became known less for cutting hair than for his feat of eating fifty raw eggs in fifteen minutes. Two hundred people gathered on Main Street as he swallowed the eggs and collected the $30 prize.

KELLOGG'S BLOCK, MAIN STREET, 1890. Mirick Spear stands in the doorway of his book and stationery shop on the right, as student boarders hang out on the building's two towers. Boarding houses were common, but few made much money. A nineteenth-century commentator noted, "One reason for the lack of success is the low price of board per week: $3.50 to $4.00, and the boarders must have the best meats, gilt-edged butter, the nicest of berries, fruit and vegetables in their season, canned fruits of all kinds, and besides all this one would suppose from the airs they put on that they were paying $20 per week, instead of the paltry sum of $3.50."

THE FIRST CONGREGATIONAL CHURCH, MAIN STREET, 1880. Built in 1867 across from the Dickinson family homes, this was the third location for the church. Emily Dickinson's brother Austin was instrumental in its erection. Emily was at her most prolific in the 1860s, writing hundreds of poems in the seclusion of her father's house. She never saw the inside of this church, but it is said she crept to the edge of her family's property to see it by moonlight.

THE AMHERST AND BELCHERTOWN RAILROAD STATION, MAIN STREET. Edward Dickinson, Emily's father, worked hard to bring the railroad through Amherst, as an economic boost to a town that didn't have the transportation advantages, like Hadley, of being located on the Connecticut River. On May 3, 1853, the first train arrived at this station from New London, Connecticut. Edward led the grand parade around town, while Emily watched from the woods before abruptly returning home. Biographer Richard Sewall described this as "a neurotic escape, a portent of stranger behaviour to come."

THE AMHERST STAGE COACH, 1870s. Seen at the Common, in front of the Amherst House, this coach carried visitors between the railroad station and the hotel. Other coaches from William Stebbins' Livery Stable connected Amherst with surrounding towns.

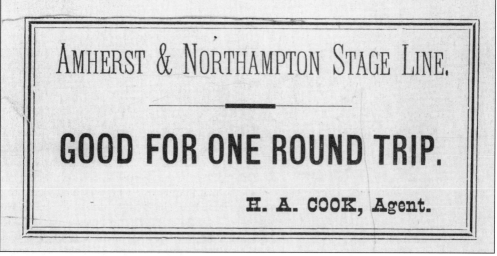

An Amherst & Northampton Stage Coach Ticket.

THE AMHERST HOUSE, SOUTH PLEASANT AND AMITY STREETS, 1879. In about 1757 Warner Tavern was built on this site, on land owned by Reverend David Parsons of First Church. When the minister died in 1781, he willed the tavern to his son, Gideon Parsons. He was followed by Joel Dickinson, who was followed as tavern keeper by Solomon Boltwood (1804), and Elijah Boltwood (1806). For more than thirty years, Boltwood Tavern was among the best known inns in western Massachusetts. In 1838, Harvey Rockwood bought the inn and changed its name to the Amherst House.

THE AMHERST HOUSE IN RUINS, JULY 4, 1879. At 1 am on the Fourth of July, 1879, one of Amherst's worst fires in history occurred. Amherst College Professor William S. Tyler wrote in his diary, "Woke up to hear and see this morning that most of the business part of the town, hotel, Post Office, Savings Bank, book stores and principal shops had been burned out during the night. We heard the bells and the noise but thought it the usual hullabaloo before the fourth, and would not open our eyes or ears but slept on. Sad sight in the morning! Common covered with wreck and the town in ruins."

THE AMHERST HOUSE FIRE, AFTERMATH, JULY 4, 1879. The Amherst Fire Company rests dispiritedly after the fire. The Common is littered with what Amherst College students were able to save from the burning buildings. Adding to the misery, poet Eugene Field, who grew up in Amherst, commented, "I fail to recognize any bliss in vegetating in that humdrum, old fogy hamlet of Amherst. When God Almight visited the place with fire, it's a pity he didn't complete the job."

THE AMHERST HOUSE, 1880. Rebuilt after the fire, the Amherst House continued to chatter with activity until it closed in 1917. In 1919, the Jones Library opened on the second floor while shops filled the street level. In 1926, the Amherst House Block, along with the library, shops, and apartments, burned down.

CANDIDA MUSANTE, 1905. John and Candida Musante, both born in Italy, sold nuts and fruits on South Pleasant Street beginning in 1882. Sometimes known as "The Peanut Fiend" (because of the number of shells his customers scattered around town), John was usually called "Peanut John." In 1896, the newspaper reported, "Mr. and Mrs. John Musante and two children have gone to Italy where they will make an extended visit. 'Peanut John's' many friends hope he will have a jolly good time and not forget to come back." After his death in 1904, Candida kept the tradition going another twenty years, until her death in 1924.

MERCHANTS ROW, SOUTH PLEASANT STREET, 1860s. This very early photograph along the west side of the Common shows the first phase of commercial building in the center of town. Low, separate business and farmhouse-style buildings existed side-by-side. Attorney Ithamar F. Conkey (town moderator, district attorney, justice of the peace, etc.), had his office on the right. J.S. & C. Adams, publishers and booksellers since 1824, had their shop in the brick building at center.

MERCHANTS ROW, SOUTH PLEASANT STREET, 1880s. An unbroken row of brick blocks was created after the fire of 1879, and most of these facades remain today. In the 1880s, Jackson & Cutler dry goods, where Emily Dickinson's family shopped, was the second shop from left. In 1888, Orson Couch brought his version of health food to Amherst in his shop on the far right. He sold Strawberry Hill Sausage and Lard, from pigs he babied with baths and a buttermilk diet.

THE FIRST BAPTIST CHURCH, SOUTH PLEASANT STREET, 1890s. Baptists first began meeting in Amherst in 1827, at the home of Stephen J. Nelson. Warren Howland, architect of some of the finest buildings in the valley, completed the church in 1836. The building was used by the congregation until 1964, when a new church was built on North Pleasant Street, near the UMass campus. Today, various businesses and a bus station occupy the old church.

SOUTH PLEASANT STREET, c. 1905. After the turn of the century, Merchants Row changed drastically. The streets along the Common were crisscrossed with trolley, electric, and phone lines. A tall flag pole was added to the Common, behind which can be seen a bandstand.

AN ACCIDENT ON THE AMHERST TROLLEY LINE, 1926. Horses would occasionally bolt and toss sleigh riders off a bridge, but the age of trolleys was no safer, as evidenced by this Amherst trolley accident on the road to Pelham.

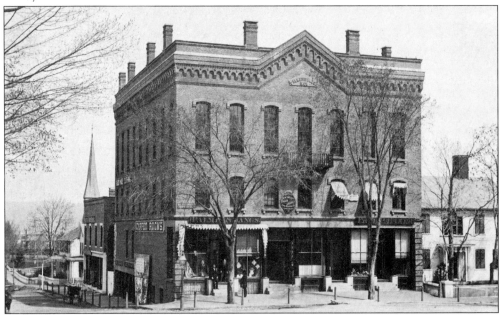

PALMER'S BLOCK, 1870s. On the opposite side of the Common from Merchants Row, lawyer Dwight Palmer built Palmer's Block in 1868. At the corner of Boltwood and Main, it was the site of town meetings, concerts, and an "opera house" for popular singers and animal acts. Above Palmer & Bangs' carpet and dry goods store was the law office of Edward Dickinson, which was continued by his son Austin. John Mullen's meat market was here, as were two Chinese laundries, one of which was run, it was said, by a woman disguised as a man to evade immigration officials.

THE AMHERST TOWN HALL. During the famous Blizzard of 1888, Palmer's Block was destroyed by fire when firefighters couldn't get through the snow. The town constructed this now classic Amherst structure, designed by H.S. McKay of Boston. Ironically, when it was built it caused some controversy. The *Amherst Record* commented, "We should bear in mind the fact that the architect of the Cathedral at Milan, backed by the wealth of the universe, could not have designed a village horse-shed that would meet with universal favor at the hands of the citizens of Amherst."

GRACE EPISCOPAL CHURCH, BOLTWOOD AVENUE, *c.* 1870. Seen from behind in this unusual photograph, Grace Church was designed by English architect Henry Dudley. Built in 1865–66, it brought the stone elegance of an English country church to the Amherst Common.

THE LORD JEFFERY INN, BOLTWOOD AVENUE, *c.* 1930. The Lord Jeff was built in 1926 by the architectural firm of Putnam & Cox. Though this whitewashed brick gem was designed all of a piece, it appears as if rooms and wings were casually added to a substantial eighteenth-century home. Two years later, the same firm added the Jones Library to the town, this time an eighteenth-century home in stone. In 1959, the inn was used in the film *Silent Night, Lonely Night*, starring Shirley Jones and Lloyd Bridges. In 1992 it was again seen in a film, *Damages*, featuring Nicole Kidman and Alec Baldwin.

ZION CHAPEL, CORNER OF WOODSIDE AVENUE AND ROUTE 9, BEFORE 1910. African-Americans attended First Church at least as early as 1742. In the 1820s, their children attended services held by Amherst College students. Zion Chapel was built for their community in 1869, with funds raised by the college faculty and townspeople. In 1910, with Moses Goodwin as chairman of the board, the congregation moved to a new African Methodist Episcopal Zion Church on Woodside Avenue.

HOPE CONGREGATIONAL CHURCH,
GAYLORD STREET, 1959. In 1912, the
members of A.M.E. Zion Church with
more Congregationalist leanings built
Hope Church. Known as the Hope
Community Church since 1967, it has
grown enormously and serves a broad
mix of worshippers.

THE HOPE CONGREGATIONAL CHURCH
DEDICATION, 1912. Many families whose
names are still familiar in Amherst
(such as Bias, Roberts, and Newport)
attended the church's dedication.

NORTH PLEASANT STREET, EARLY 1870s. The center of Amherst was lined with elegant elms until the Hurricane of 1938. September of that year had been the wettest in sixty-seven years. When the hurricane struck, with gusts up to 120 miles an hour, more than 2,000 trees were uprooted, thrown across roads, and dashed into houses. Ironically, in 1925 Frederick Law Olmsted had told Amherst College that replanting their haphazard landscaping was out of the question "unless some calamity should destroy all the trees at one fell swoop."

NORTH PLEASANT STREET, EAST SIDE, *c.* 1895. Sanderson's Clothing Store (right) seems to have started the sidewalk sales tradition that continues today on this same street. Next to Sanderson's was the Grange Store, begun by the local grange in 1877, then run by Mason A. Dickinson and his sons for over fifty years. In 1885 a bomb set by "professional cracksmen," as they were called, ripped open the store's safe in a daring robbery.

THE GRANGE STORE, NORTH PLEASANT STREET. After the turn of the century, canned fruits and vegetables were added to local produce at the Grange Store. From left to right are Mr. and Mrs. Mason Dickinson, Frank Loomis, John Donahue, Mason A. Dickinson Jr., and Tom Smith.

NORTH PLEASANT STREET, WEST SIDE, *c.* 1920. Trolley tracks, cars, and horses illustrate the jumble of transportation modes of the time. They're seen in front of Wiley's Livery Stable, the fire station (center), and a Ford dealership.

THE ALERT HOSE COMPANY, #1, 1880s. Until 1838 firefighting was done by volunteers who supplied their own equipment. Then the town bought "cataract engines," which took at least eight men to pull and were operated by hand pumps. In 1846, the Lafayette Hook and Ladder Company met at Howe's Hotel for the first time. Their main order of business was to elect a commissary general, who "when called upon to administer to his toiling comrades should pour forth the indomitable and invincible spirit which will gladden their hearts while combating the raging elements."

SAINT BRIGID'S CHURCH, NORTH PLEASANT STREET. The Northern Italian design of St. Brigid's adds terra-cotta and yellow brick to the New England white of much of the rest of the town. John Slater, born in Ireland in 1803, may have been the first Catholic in Amherst. He arrived at a time when, as was said, "Amherst had a charm for all but the Catholic." Later Irish and Polish immigration to the area helped this and other Catholic churches thrive.

S.K. ORR, DRUGS, MEDICINES, CHEMICALS, CORNER OF AMITY AND NORTH PLEASANT STREETS, 1859. One of the earliest photographs of the top of Amity Street (at the north end of the Common), this shows Dr. Field in his wagon in front of Orr's apothecary shop. Emily Dickinson's brother Austin stands at the rear wheel.

CHASE'S BLOCK, CORNER OF AMITY AND NORTH PLEASANT STREETS, 1894. S.K. Orr's apothecary shop had also housed the post office, Carter and Adams printing office, *The New England Inquirer*, and the American Express and Western Union Telegraph offices. William Gunn opened a hotel here in 1877, adding a hipped roof to the old building. The popular Frank P. Wood took over the hotel in 1882, and was followed by Lorenzo Chase in 1892.

AMITY STREET, 1880s. William Gunn's hotel (1877) is on right. His career, unfortunately, was checkered with lawsuits for bad debts and arrests for selling liquor without a license. The *Amherst Record*, angry about the ban on liquor sales in Amherst, came to his defense: "No one in town is known to have entered complaint against the proprietor of Gunn's hotel, and it looks like a detestable piece of business for a state officer to send his spies around the country to spy out fraud, and rely on fraud for evidence, whether the accused parties are guilty or not."

DINNER.

Sunday 18

June 13th 1880

SOUP.

Rice

BOILED.

Fricassee Chicken Cranberry Sauce

ROAST.

LOIN BEEF. Brown Sauce

Baked Stuffed Lamb

VEGETABLES.

BOILED POTATOES.   MASHED POTATOES.

Green Peas

Squash   Turnip

RELISHES.

FRENCH MUSTARD.   TOMATO CATSUP.   HORSE RADISH.

WORCESTERSHIRE SAUCE.   CHOW CHOW.

OLIVES.   CHEESE.   PICKLES.

Cucumbers Spiced Tomatoes Onions

PUDDINGS.

Tapioca

PASTRY.

MINCE PIE.   APPLE PIE.

Custard Pie   Rhubarb Pie

ICE CREAM.   ICES.

Strawberry

TEA.   COFFEE.

DESSERT.

BILL OF FARE, GUNN'S HOTEL, JUNE 13, 1880. This is a typical menu for Sunday dinner at Gunn's, featuring chicken fricassee, rice soup, cranberry sauce, roast beef, baked stuffed lamb, squash, peas, turnips, cucumbers, spiced tomatoes, onions, tapioca pudding, custard and rhubarb pies, strawberry ice cream, nuts, and raisins.

PARISEAU BLOCK, AMITY STREET, 1920s. Located here were the American Railway Express office, W.B. Drury's Bakery, J.B. Bement's Coal and Wood, and Vincent Grandonico's Shoe Repairing (Shoe Dying a Specialty). This and the surrounding buildings were removed in 1927 for the building of the Jones Library.

THE JONES LIBRARY, AMITY STREET, 1940s. Samuel Minot Jones left his lumber fortune to his son Minot, with the stipulation that should he not survive to assume the estate it would be used for a town library. Minot died during World War I, and the Jones Library was established in the Amherst House hotel in 1919. After the Amherst House burned down in 1926, a handsome new building was designed by Putnam and Cox of Boston. Anthony Rufo (nicknamed Michelangelo) and his crew of Italian craftsmen built the library from stone gathered from mill sites in Pelham and Granby.

THE STRONG HOUSE, AMITY STREET, 1880s. Nehemiah Strong built this house, which he deeded to his son Simeon in the 1760s. During the Revolution, lawyer Simeon Strong used his house as headquarters for the local Tories. Later, during the Emerson family's ownership (1853–1916), poet Eugene Field wrote this verse about his dog Dooley: "O, had I wings like a dove I would fly/Away from this world of fleas/I'd fly all around Miss Emerson's yard/And light on Miss Emerson's trees."

PAIGE'S LIVERY STABLE AND THE AMITY STREET SCHOOL, 1880s. The stable, built in 1880 by William Stebbins, was owned by the Paige family from 1883 to 1921. Like many stablemen, the Paiges went into the automobile business. Few of the students who today see films in this building realize it began as a livery stable.

AMHERST ACADEMY, AMITY STREET, 1860s. Noah Webster, Samuel Fowler Dickinson (Emily's grandfather), and others founded Amherst Academy in 1814. An excellent preparatory school, students included Mary Lyon (founder of Mount Holyoke College), Emily Dickinson, and Sylvester Graham. The latter was known as "The Philosopher of Sawdust Pudding" for his advocacy of whole grain Graham flour, which led to today's graham crackers.

Two
East Amherst:
Dissent and a Shifting Center

NORTH EAST STREET FROM EAST AMHERST COMMON, 1860s. East Amherst was likely the first area in town settled. Tradition says a Mr. Foote built a shanty here prior to 1703. After the Revolution, East Amherst developed as the center of town. Town meetings were held here, and stage coaches brought the first mail to the postmaster's house. Dry goods stores, tanneries, shoemakers, and substantial factories that produced carriages, tools (particularly planes), and hats were located here before the center shifted to its present location.

THE SECOND CONGREGATIONAL CHURCH, MAIN STREET, EAST AMHERST, *c.* 1905. In 1783, a Second Congregational Parish was organized after a dissident group objected to Tory sympathizer Reverend David Parsons III at First Church. Built in 1839 by architect Warren S. Howland, the building is now the home of the Jewish Community of Amherst.

THE EBENEZER MATTOON HOUSE, SOUTH EAST STREET, EAST AMHERST, *c.* 1905. Built about 1782, and still standing, this was the home of Ebenezer Mattoon—the Revolutionary War hero, Amherst legislator, justice of the peace, sheriff, state senator, and Congressman.

THE FIRST NATIONAL BANK, MAIN STREET, 1860s. The First National Bank was chartered in 1863 and built by noted local architect William Fenno Pratt. In the eastern part of town, it was nearby a grocery store (far left), a druggist (in same building), Sisson's Hotel, the railroad station, and the Hills Hat Factory.

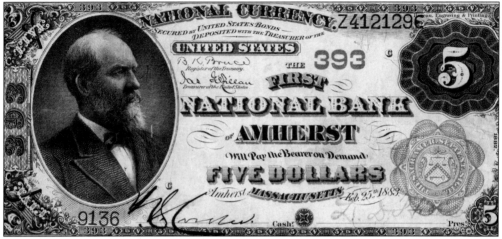

FIRST NATIONAL BANK CURRENCY, 1883. Like most banks, Amherst's First National issued its own currency, such as this $5 bill.

THE HILLS HAT CO., MAIN STREET, *c.* 1910. Leonard M. Hills started making palm leaf hats in East Amherst after moving there from Connecticut in 1829. By 1855 his company made more than half of all such hats in the country. The Hills Company built its substantial factory, and the family's two mansions, by the railroad station between East Amherst and Amherst Center, as commercial development shifted in that direction.

HENRY JACKSON, 1870s. Born in 1818, Henry Jackson was schooled in East Amherst, where he cornered the freight hauling business in town. He handled goods in his buckboard, taking palm leaf hats and other local products to distant train lines, and carrying local business deposits to Northampton and Greenfield banks, before banking was fully established in town. One famous episode among many in Jackson's life occurred in 1840, when he helped save Angeline Palmer from being abducted into slavery.

CHARLES E. JACKSON, 1880s. Henry Jackson's son Charles followed briefly in his father's footsteps. His obituary in 1891 reads, "Charles E. Jackson, who for a number of years has assisted his father in the trucking business, died at his home on Whitney Street, aged 28 years. He had been sick for some two weeks and death was caused by gastritis complicated with heart trouble. Funeral services were held on Sunday at Zion Chapel and were largely attended . . . Mr. Jackson leaves a widow, who with his aged parents have the sympathy of the community in their affliction."

Three
South Amherst:
Fiddlers' Green, Children's Carriages,
and the Poor Farm

THE SHUMWAY FARM AND SOUTH AMHERST, 1932. South East and Shays Streets were laid out in 1759, forming a crossroads in the south of town and a nexus for a village. For generations, a Native American trail ran along the foot of Mount Holyoke between Hadley and Brookfield. This became Bay Road, a military supply route later used as part of the stage route connecting Boston and Albany.

he Church and Street, South Amherst, Mass.

SOUTH AMHERST COMMON, 1910. In 1788, Amherst set aside a common here for public use, thus recognizing South Amherst as a distinct village within the town. Called "Fiddlers' Green" for the fiddling contests held on it during the nineteenth century, it was soon surrounded by shops and the homes of prosperous farmers. In 1825, George Nutting and Philip Goss built the South Congregational Church on land given by Nathaniel Dickinson. An aggressive rivalry between singers in the choir led to a bitter split in 1859. Two congregations met on two floors of the same church, and though the church eventually reunited, friction lasted for more than a generation.

THE SOUTH AMHERST POST OFFICE AND GROCERY, MIDDLE STREET AND POMEROY LANE, 1880s. The South Amherst Post Office began in this house in 1841, and was usually run in conjunction with a dry goods or grocery store. Charles J. King was the last postmaster here in 1932.

THE AMHERST POOR FARM, SOUTH AMHERST COMMON, 1880s. In 1836, the town purchased Medad Vinton's farm on the South Amherst Common and hired a warden, a doctor, and a minister to watch over the town's poor. The "inmates," as they were called, included vagrants and the mentally unstable. The town also supported Amherst's poor families if they lived out of town: "Our outside poor are a great expense to the town and trouble to the overseers. In case of sickness with these persons who are living away from the Alms House, the expense is likely to be great." The Poor Farm was burned down by a resident in 1882, but was rebuilt. It closed in 1914.

THE SOUTH AMHERST SCHOOL HOUSE, 1896. To the left of this one-room schoolhouse can be seen the outhouse and the wood pile for the stove. Teacher Alice Marsh stands to the left of her pupils, who represent a cross-section of South Amherst families: the Shumways, Dwights, Morells, Girards, and, of course, Dickinsons.

THE MILL VALLEY SCHOOL, SOUTH AMHERST, 1890. Serving families that lived near Fort River, this small school was led by teacher Grace Phillips. To her left was Bessie Holley. The others are as follows: (front row) Nellie Merrick, Daisy Clay, Will Kellogg, and Raymond Stowell; (second row) Bradford Brown, Walter Kellogg, and Lena Bias.

A MILL VALLEY GRISTMILL, 1890s. By the 1740s, sawmills and gristmills appeared along the Mill River in South Amherst. This one, the Simeon Clark gristmill, dates from about 1790. Bought in 1903 by Alfred Sanctuary, it was still run as a mill in 1938. Since then it has been a restaurant and an antiques shop.

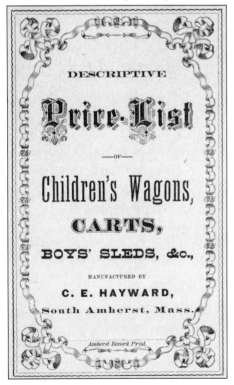

C.E. HAYWARD, CHILDREN'S WAGONS, CARTS, AND SLEDS. The Hayward family began making children's carriages in South Amherst in 1845. They expanded to wagons, carts, and sleds for children as competing factories were begun. In 1865, there were three such factories, producing 17,750 children's carriages and sleds each year.

THE MUNSON MEMORIAL LIBRARY, SEEN FROM A SOUTH CONGREGATIONAL CHURCH WINDOW. Mary A. Munson left money for a library in 1915. Fifteen years later this charming brick building, with fine woodworking and fireplaces, became the community center for South Amherst.

WHITCOMB'S BLACKSMITH SHOP, SOUTH EAST STREET, c. 1905. For less money than a skilled carpenter or mason could make, the blacksmith suffered extreme heat, noise, and dangerous kicks from his clients. Whitcomb seems to have earned a few extra pennies by advertising Magic Yeast, Sanderson & Thompson's Clothing, and Mandell's Shoe Store. The sign on right reads, "DO YOU COUGH DON'T DELAY TAKE KEMP'S BALSAM THE BEST COUGH CURE."

THE AMHERST BRICK COMPANY, SOUTH EAST STREET, 1900. Four brickyards in Amherst sold bricks throughout southern New England. One of the earliest brick homes in Amherst was built for Emily Dickinson's family in 1813. This brickyard was begun in 1886, and was conveniently located between the two Amherst railroad lines.

Four
North Amherst:
Mills, Peddlers, and an Organ Grinder

NORTH AMHERST, MONTAGUE ROAD, LOOKING SOUTH, c. 1905. Children play by the trolley tracks, with North Amherst Center in the background. North Amherst owes its early development to the Mill River. The first mill in Amherst was built here after Hadley "granted to Nathaniel Kellogg liberty to erect a saw mill on Mill river at the place called the biggest falls" on March 3, 1740.

THE NORTH CONGREGATIONAL CHURCH, 1890s. Most settlers in North Amherst had attended the Second Congregational Church in East Amherst until November 15, 1826, when they established this church under most unusual circumstances. The meetinghouse was built through the zeal and funding of Oliver Dickinson, on land donated by Joseph Cowles. Dickinson considered himself sole owner of the church and determined where it would be built and how it was built. He stipulated that pews could not be owned or occupied by any "negro or mulatto."

NORTH AMHERST, LOOKING WEST ON MEADOW STREET, 1870s. Joseph Cowles built the brick house on the left in 1821 on land bought by his father David. The elder Cowles was the town's hogreeve, tithingman, constable, surveyor of highways, and commissioner. On the right is the A.B. Cloud dry goods store, later owned by Frank N. Dickinson.

THE FRANK N. DICKINSON STORE, NORTH AMHERST, 1920. Dickinson, born in North Amherst in 1866, bought this store from A.B. Cloud in about 1898. At the same time, Frank's brother, Mason A. Dickinson, was running the Grange Store in Amherst Center. Here, standing by the gas pumps, are Raymond Bates and Earl Ottinger.

THE FRANK N. DICKINSON STORE, NORTH AMHERST, *c.* 1900. Henry Stetson sits on the steps of the Dickinson Store, which apparently sold a lot of Moxie soda. The store was later the Bates Store; in the 1970s and early 1980s it was Watroba's.

THE NORTH AMHERST SCHOOL, NORTH SIDE OF CLOUD'S GENERAL STORE, 1880s. The first school in North Amherst was built in 1771. Several wooden schoolhouses later, this solid brick school was built in 1870.

The North Amherst Post Office, *c*. 1905. A.B. Cloud moved his general store across the street in about 1898. On the right a shop sold groceries and tobaccos, while the post office was on the left. Here, postmaster Forester Ainsworth held seances and communicated with the dead through automatic writing.

Factory Hollow Pond,
North Amherst, Mass.

FACTORY HOLLOW, NORTH AMHERST, c. 1910. The number of mills along the Mill River led to this area being called Factory Hollow. Here, for example, Ebenezer Dickinson built a three-story cotton yarn factory in 1809. After a series of bad debts and lawsuits, Dickinson broke into the factory, stole a quantity of cotton yarn, and left for Ohio, hurling a curse on the Hollow as he left. His curse may or may not have been responsible for the burning of the cotton and woolen mills on the river in 1842, 1847, 1851, and 1857.

PUFFER'S GRISTMILL, MONTAGUE ROAD, 1890s. Originally built in 1838, this gristmill was owned and operated by the Stephen Puffer family from 1844 to 1934.

A PAPER MILL ON MILL RIVER, BETWEEN NORTH AMHERST AND CUSHMAN. Papermaking, one of Amherst's first industries, began at least as early as 1795. It continued for nearly a century until South Hadley and Holyoke, with better water power and transportation, surpassed Amherst.

THE NORTH AMHERST LIBRARY, 1893. The library (built in 1893), and P.L. Dowd's blacksmith shop next to it, sit at the crossroads of North Amherst. Edith Hardendorff, who became the librarian in 1904, saw a lot from here. She remembered the medicine peddler who talked through ventriloquism to his friend Pedro in the library's coal bin. An Italian organ grinder and his monkey passed in front of the library once, as did a man and his dancing bear. While sleeping in a barn with his "pet," the bear supposedly woke up hungry and ate his owner.

Five

Cushman:
Taverns, Paper Making,
and Death by Boiling Bleach

THE JOHN AND MARTHA GERMAIN STORE, PINE STREET, CUSHMAN, *c.* 1920. In 1759, as Amherst was set off as a district of Hadley, John Adams bought land in the northeast part of town and built a small mill. Called North Amherst City, and sometimes simply "The City," it was named for the Cushman family in 1930. This store, owned by the Germains from 1919 to 1930, was begun as Cogswell's Store in about 1896, and is still run as a general store today.

L.L. Draper's Tavern, Bridge Street, Cushman, 1866. As early as 1818, Rufus Kellogg was a licensed innkeeper, and kept a tavern in this building. He sold the place to Leprelate Draper, and it is probably his son, Lewis L. Draper, who is seen here.

Avery R. Cushman's "Red Mill," 1898–99. The Cushman family produced paper, strawboard, and leatherboard here between 1835 and 1902. While other Amherst papermakers lost business to larger towns, the Cushmans diversified by inventing a wrapping paper made from bleached straw and rye stalks, and a synthetic leather made from leather scraps and old rope. This, one of two Cushman mills, stood close to the corner of State Street and Leverett Road. From left to right are Moses Cushman, Luther Crossman, Walter Warren, Fred Wood, Alfred Clark, and John Hardaker.

PAPER MAKER REUBEN ROBERTS, EARLY 1860s. The Reuben Roberts family owned two paper mills on Mill River, the first having been bought in 1806. In 1849, Reuben's son Sylvester was bleaching straw in a large cauldron when a rope snapped and he tumbled into the boiling bleach. Only three months earlier, Sylvester's eighteen-month-old son William had died by scalding in the same mill.

THE BUNGHOLE BELOW CUSHMAN BRIDGE, 1890s. This is a rare stereoview of a site on Mill River once known as The Forge (where "frogs" for railroad tracks were forged), and later as The Bunghole. The Cushman family's large Red Mill is in the background.

THE NORTH CITY PRIMARY SCHOOL, 1888–89. Ella L. Roberts, seen here in a stylish hat, taught at this one-room schoolhouse in Cushman. Among her students were Sadie Spear, Sadie Hardaker, Edith Heald, Emma Tracy, Ellis Harlow, Edmund Wilbur, Susan F. Wilson, George Spear, Mary Ashley, and Belle Roberts.

Six

Business and Pleasure:

Baseball, Factory Whistles,
and the Roar of the Fourth

THE PHOENIX ROW BASEBALL TEAM OF 1892. By 1890, the clerks on Merchants Row (South Pleasant Street) were involved in a heated rivalry with those on Phoenix Row (Main Street). After Merchants Row lost the 1892 game, the team brought in ringers from other parts of town. Phoenix Row objected, arguments flew back and forth, and the game was nearly canceled. But the crowds came, some with homemade root beer from the Grange Store, others with Hood's Sarsaparilla from Deuel's Drug Store. Merchants Row beat Phoenix Row handily.

THE AMHERST BICYCLE CLUB, MAY 16, 1881. This early club led to the Wheelmen of Amherst and the Nonotuck Bicycle Club in 1889. Bicycling became a great craze in the 1890s. The new form of transport caused so much confusion in the streets that it was labeled "the deadly bicycle," and those that rode them were "bicycle fiends." Bicycle races were held on the Fourth of July at Hampshire Park on Belchertown Road, but most preferred watching horses race to the lesser excitements of primitive bicycles.

HOLLAND & GALLOND DRY GOODS, PAINTS, AND OILS, PHOENIX ROW, 1890s. The members of the losing Phoenix Row baseball team are, from left to right, George Gaskill, George Gallond, Harry Holland, Leander Merrick, and Benjamin Avery.

BOOKSELLER MIRICK N. SPEAR AND FRIENDS, 1860s. Groucho Marx once said, "Outside of a dog, a book is man's best friend. Inside of a dog, it's too dark to read." Amherst's love of books and bookstores goes back at least to Mirick Spear, who ran his bookstore from 1849 to his death in 1899. To the far left is Attorney Ithamar F. Conkey, and in the center is Lem Coe, an engineer on the Amherst and Belchertown Railroad.

A GENT AT MORGAN'S DRUGSTORE, 1880s. An unidentified gentleman sits at the soda fountain of Morgan's Drugstore on Phoenix Row, Main Street. William Henry Harrison Morgan owned the store from 1880 to 1909.

MACHINIST AND INVENTOR EDMUND A. THOMPSON, AFTER 1895. Known locally mostly as a town tinker, Thompson repaired anything from tin whistles to sensitive German optics, and accompanied Amherst College astronomer David Todd on expeditions to Japan and Tripoli. He worked out of a shop behind the Baptist church on the Common. In 1912, Amherst College conferred upon him an honorary Master of Science Degree.

THE AMAZING PHONO-ELECTRO-POLYMOBILICON, 1906. In a parody of the wonders of the new century, the First Congregational Church held a demonstration of this strange contraption. Adding deadpan humor to the event were estimable hat factory owner William Burnett (fourth from left, standing) and Edmund Thompson (standing, far right).

JOHN MULLEN'S MEATS AND PROVISIONS, SOUTH PLEASANT STREET, AFTER 1914. John Mullen (left) presided over barrels of apples, potatoes, and onions, tubs of butter, and an entire pig, hanging in the background.

THE WORLD'S ALL RIGHT, AUGUST 1, 1934. During a hot summer when people in Amherst were occupied with bird watching, bean-counting, and dancing in the town's first refrigerated ballroom, the Amherst Grange was inspired to produce a wacky musical called The World's All Right, which had many notable locals cross-dressing on Pratt Field.

THE HILLS HAT FACTORY, COLLEGE AND RAILROAD STREETS, *c.* 1905. When Leonard M. Hills began making palm leaf hats in Amherst in 1829, it was a simple process. Women wove hats on their farms and Hills sold them from a shop. By the end of the century the Hills family had the largest palm leaf hat factory in the country.

THE HENRY D. FEARING HAT FACTORY, RAILROAD STREET, 1880s. H.D. Fearing and Company began in 1872. Between the Hills and Fearing factories nearly six hundred men and women were employed. This part of town (between the Center and East Amherst) became a thriving area with shops, the Union Hotel, and the First National Bank.

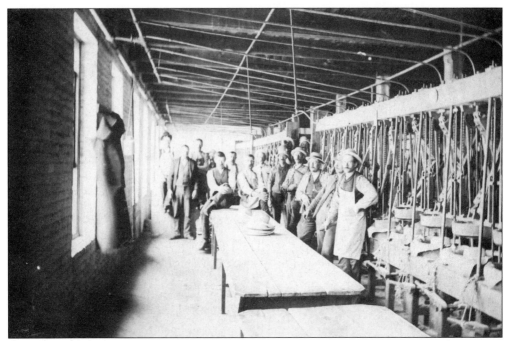

BURNETT HAT FACTORY WORKERS, 1890s. George B. Burnett & Son bought out the Fearing Company in 1892. Competition between the Burnett and Hills factories erupted into a feud in 1897. Hills workers hijacked a train that Burnett workers had hired as transportation to a company banquet in Springfield. At the banquet the Hills people stole the ice cream, broke windows, and tossed in a "stinck-pot.," causing "an intolerable stench."

WOMEN WORKERS IN THE SEWING ROOM OF THE BURNETT HAT COMPANY, 1890s. Each of the two major hat factories employed about three hundred people, with women outnumbering men two to one. They earned from $9 to $15 for a fifty-eight-hour week, and many suffered lung disease from the dust produced during the hat-making process.

WOMEN OUTSIDE THE BURNETT HAT FACTORY, 1890s. Amherst factories hired women and men born locally, while those in the eastern part of the state relied on Irish, French, and Polish immigrants. In 1905, when the Hills Company planned to run its factory completely with Japanese immigrants, women workers walked out, shutting down the factory. Their strike was successful, and the company went on for another thirty years.

THE 1899 INDEPENDENCE DAY PARADE. In 1781 Massachusetts was the first state to vote official recognition of the Fourth of July. Typically, bells rang, thirteen-gun salutes were fired, bands played, and bonfires roared. Prayers and patriotic orations were heartfelt and long. A century later, however, things changed.

INDEPENDENCE DAY ON THE AMHERST COMMON, 1890s. By the end of the century, the Fourth was kicked off by a parade of the "Resistless Battalion of Antiques and Horribles," consisting of wildly costumed "floodwoods and riffraffs" on decorated wagons. Papers took to describing the day as "an old Roman Saturnalia . . . a senseless, aimless, crash, bang, squish, roar, ding-dong, hurrah."

HERBERT THOMPSON AND FRIENDS IN SWIMWEAR, 1921. Today, swimmers still use old mill ponds, like Puffer's Pond, in hot weather. In the nineteenth century, if swimming was done publicly at all, it was done in primitive gear. One magazine said, "Some wear bloomers, some are wrapped in crimson Turkish dressing gowns and flounder through waves like long-legged flamingoes. Others wear old pantaloons and worn out jackets."

Seven

Writers and Poets:
"A Lively Interest in Thought Everywhere"
—Mary Heaton Vorse

A WOODCUT OF EMILY DICKINSON (1830–1886) BY ERIC DAVIS.

EMILY DICKINSON, PEN AND INK BY BARRY MOSER, 1976. Emily Elizabeth Dickinson was born on Main Street in Amherst in 1830. Historian Robert A. Gross has written, "Emily Dickinson commands an international reputation as a major American poet, but her person remains surrounded by legend and mystery. To many, she is simply a half-mad recluse, nursing her disappointments in eccentric, heart-broken spiritual rebellion against the conformity of her age . . . She knew herself better . . . In the 1,775 poems she left behind, she laid bare the inner doubts and passionate longings with which an exceptionally sensitive New Englander could enter the modern world."

THE DICKINSON HOMESTEAD, LITHOGRAPH BY JOHN BACHELDER, 1855–56. The brick Homestead was built in 1813 for the poet's grandfather, Samuel Fowler Dickinson. The elder Dickinson helped found Amherst College, but lost a fortune in the process. In 1830, he rented half the house to his son Edward.

THE NORTH PLEASANT STREET DICKINSON HOUSE. In 1833, Samuel Fowler Dickinson left Amherst, bankrupt. He sold his half of the Homestead to the Mack family. Meanwhile, Edward sold his own half of the house, but stayed as a renter until he bought this large white house on North Pleasant Street in 1840.

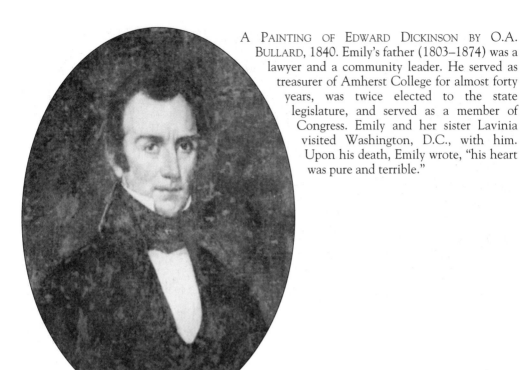

A Painting of Edward Dickinson by O.A. Bullard, 1840. Emily's father (1803–1874) was a lawyer and a community leader. He served as treasurer of Amherst College for almost forty years, was twice elected to the state legislature, and served as a member of Congress. Emily and her sister Lavinia visited Washington, D.C., with him. Upon his death, Emily wrote, "his heart was pure and terrible."

A Painting of Emily Norcross Dickinson by O.A. Bullard, 1840. Well educated and from a prominent family in the nearby town of Monson, Emily Norcross (1804–1882) suffered ill health and was cared for in later years by her daughters. After her death, Emily wrote, "the dear mother that could not walk has flown."

A Postcard of the Dickinson Homestead, Main Street, c. 1910. In 1855, after Edward Dickinson was firmly established, he bought the old Homestead and moved his family back to Main Street. The house was expanded and a conservatory was added where Emily could grow flowers and herbs.

The Dickinson Homestead Interior, c. 1946. A chair belonging to the poet is in front of the fireplace, ornately carved with grapevines.

Austin Dickinson, *c.* 1845. Austin, Emily's brother, was a lawyer, town moderator, and, after his father's death, treasurer of Amherst College. Hardly anyone in Emily's life was as close to her as her brother. In later years, she wrote to him, "I wish we were children now. I wish we were always children, how to grow up I dont know."

Lavinia Dickinson, June 1896. It was Emily's sister Lavinia who found hundreds of Emily's poems in a bureau after the poet's death. Emily had never kept the fact that she wrote poetry secret; the surprise was the shear volume of extraordinary work. Lavinia's passion was to see her sister's poetry in print. Another passion was stray cats, some of whom she named Tabby, Drummydoodles, Buffy, and Tootsie.

THE EVERGREENS, MAIN STREET, *c.* 1920. After Austin's marriage to Susan Gilbert on July 1, 1856, the couple moved into an elegant Italianate house next door to the family Homestead. Many Amherst College commencement teas were held here, and many prominent visitors were entertained. The marriage was unhappy, however. Of their three children, Gib died tragically at the age of eight, and neither Ned nor Mattie had children. Thus, the Edward Dickinson line ended here.

SUSAN GILBERT DICKINSON, *c.* 1850. Though Susan's relationship with Emily Dickinson later became problematic, for many years she and Emily were very close and Emily called her "Sister Sue." Emotionally charged letters passed between the two houses, and Emily valued Sue's opinions of her poems.

THE PATH BETWEEN THE DICKINSON HOUSES, MAIN STREET. Though Emily Dickinson gradually became a recluse, she did, for the most part, cross this path to her brother's house. Today, the Dickinson Homestead is open to the public, and Austin's house, The Evergreens, is being restored for future viewing.

EMILY DICKINSON'S GRAVE SITE, WEST CEMETERY. On May 15, 1886, the poet died in her bed on the second floor of the Homestead. Her casket was carried, at her request, by the Irish workmen who cared for the family home. She was taken out the back door, through the barn, and across the fields to the old town cemetery. Thomas Wentworth Higginson wrote that she "looked 30, not a gray hair or wrinkle, and perfect peace (was) on the beautiful brow. There was a little bunch of violets at the neck . . . the sister Vinnie put in two heliotropes by her hand."

ROBERT FROST AT THE HOME OF POET ROBERT FRANCIS, AMHERST, 1956. "Robert Frost first came to Amherst to reside in 1916, having just returned from England with his newly acquired fame, like a crisp and ripening apple, in his pocket. It took our village a little while to become used to him . . . Meanwhile eloquent years were coming and going. Mr. Frost has maintained his intermittent but ever recurring residence in our little town." —From an Address by Frank Prentice Rand, The Jones Library, 1959.

THE ROBERT FROST HOUSE, SUNSET AVENUE, AMHERST, 1936. Frost taught, lectured, and read at Amherst College between 1916 and his last appearance there on October 19, 1960. Robert and Elinor Frost bought this house in 1931. It was sold in 1938 after the unexpected death of Elinor.

PRESIDENT JOHN F. KENNEDY AT THE AMHERST COMMON, OCTOBER 26, 1963. Robert Frost died on January 29, 1963. The following October, Amherst College held groundbreaking ceremonies for the Robert Frost Library. President Kennedy spoke at the event, one of his last appearance before his assassination. Of Frost, Kennedy said, ". . . because he knew the midnight as well as the high noon, because he understood the ordeal as well as the triumph of the human spirit, he gave his age strength with which to overcome despair."

ROBERT FRANCIS, 1976. Born in Pennsylvania in 1901, Robert Francis moved to Amherst in 1926 and devoted his life to writing poetry. He went from being called "the best neglected poet" by Robert Frost, to being honored with a fellowship for distinguished poetic achievement by the Academy of American Poets, as Frost had been.

FORT JUNIPER, 1940s. Robert Francis was twenty-five when he came to Amherst. "Fourteen years later," he said, "my one-man, but not one-room cottage, Fort Juniper, was built in what had been a cow pasture on the outskirts of Amherst . . . for better or for worse, I was a poet and there was really nothing else for me to do but go on being a poet . . . Poetry was my most central, intense and inwardly rewarding experience."

HELEN HUNT JACKSON, "AMHERST'S OTHER WOMAN POET." Born in 1830, the same year as Emily Dickinson, Helen Hunt Jackson became one of the most popular poets of her day. Her novel *Ramona* has been made into a film several times. *A Century of Dishonor* was an impassioned treatise on the abuse of Native Americans.

THE BIRTHPLACE OF HELEN HUNT JACKSON, OFF LESSEY STREET. Though Jackson left Amherst, she corresponded with Emily Dickinson, and was the only contemporary writer to have recognized Dickinson's genius. "You are a great poet," she wrote in 1876, "and it was wrong to the day you live in, that you will not sing aloud."

WEBSTER'S UNABRIDGED DICTIONARY.

The National Standard.

N Webster

"The Schoolmaster of the Republic."

GET THE BEST.

FOR SALE BY YOUR BOOKSELLER.---SEE LAST PAGE.

NOAH WEBSTER. Main Street had been the home of another great American writer, before the birth of Emily Dickinson. Noah Webster moved to Amherst in 1812 to work on his great unabridged dictionary. (The story goes that he reached the letter "h" while in Amherst.) Webster kept an orchard and became involved in town affairs. He and Emily Dickinson's grandfather were prime movers in the founding of Amherst College.

EUGENE FIELD, POET AND COLUMNIST. Born in St. Louis in 1850, Field was sent to live in Amherst at the age of six, after his mother died. He grew up on Amity Street, and later returned to the midwest. He became famous for his children's poems, including "Little Boy Blue," and "Wynken, Blynken, and Nod," and his newspaper column, "Sharps and Flats." Field died in 1895 while working on *The Love Affairs of a Bibliomaniac*.

RAY STANNARD BAKER, JOURNALIST, BIOGRAPHER, AND ESSAYIST. Born in 1870, Baker was a pioneering investigative journalist. He covered turn-of-the-century labor battles, and wrote *Following the Color Line*, one of the first books to uncover the sad state of race relations in both the South and the North. Woodrow Wilson asked Baker to serve as head of the American Press Corps at the World War I Peace Conference, and Baker's biography of Wilson won the Pulitzer Prize in 1940.

THE RAY STANNARD BAKER HOUSE, SUNSET AVENUE. Baker moved to Amherst in 1910, where, under the pseudonym "David Grayson," he wrote graceful books on country life. His books like *Adventures in Contentment* and *Under My Elm* became so popular that no fewer than six "David Grayson" impostors toured the country. When one proposed to a young woman, Baker decided it was time to reveal that he was the one and only "David Grayson."

MARY HEATON VORSE (RIGHT) WITH HER DAUGHTER ERNESTINE, 1924. Vorse, born in Amherst in 1870, was an international labor journalist and activist. In 1902 she marched with women strikers in Venice, and ten years later she covered the famous Lawrence, Massachusetts, textile strike. In 1937, Vorse was wounded by gunfire while covering a steel strike in Youngstown, Ohio. Of Amherst, she wrote, "There was a lively interest in thought everywhere. It was the prelude toward a wide questioning of a system which placed profits above people."

Eight
The Colleges:
Ministers, Farmers, Thinkers, and Idealists

AMHERST COLLEGE, ENGRAVING, 1855. The Trustees of Amherst Academy, with the funding and enthusiasm of men like Samuel Fowler Dickinson and Noah Webster, founded Amherst College in 1821. It was established for the classical education of "indigent and pious young men." Ralph Waldo Emerson wrote, "The infant college is an infant Hercules . . . Never was (there) so much striving, outstretching and advancing in a literary cause as is exhibited here . . ."

Amherst College from the South End of the Amherst Common, 1870s. Johnson Chapel, with its clock tower, is a central landmark. In 1823, Ralph Waldo Emerson noted in his journal, "A poor one-legged man (Adam Johnson) died last week in Pelham, who was not known to have any property, and left 4000 dollars to be appropriated to the building of a Chapel, over whose door is to be inscribed his name . . ." Johnson's brother sued Samuel Fowler Dickinson, and others, for taking advantage of his brother. He lost the case, and bequeathed Amherst "nothing but woes and maledictions."

AMHERST COLLEGE MUSICIANS, 1861. When the Class of 1860 decided to haze the freshmen of 1861, they bought a mammoth squirt gun. After being drenched, the Class of 1861 captured the gun. They held a funeral for it, played a dirge on their instruments, and laid it out in a coffin. The Class of 1860 attacked "in the greatest state of phrenzy," until College President William Stearns intervened. Most of the students went on to distinguished careers in the ministry, education, and law.

SABRINA, IN A RARE APPEARANCE AT AMHERST COLLEGE. The statue of Sabrina has been kidnapped repeatedly and cleverly since it was given to the college by local factory owner Joel Hayden. She has been abducted by competing Amherst College classes, disguised, hidden, and buried, only to surface periodically to taunt the classes looking for her. Sabrina was recently seen in a helicopter hovering over an Amherst/Williams football game.

AMHERST COLLEGE STUDENTS DRESSED FOR THE SILLY SEASON, 1896. In the spring of 1896, the streets of Amherst were described this way: "The silly season has set in with the Amherst College seniors. They are driving hoops and spinning tops and rolling marbles and playing horse like the kindergarten pupils. There may be some deep significance in this child's play, but to the uninitiated there is little to commend it."

MASSACHUSETTS AGRICULTURAL COLLEGE, ENGRAVING, 1867. In 1862, Congress passed the Morrill Land Grant Act setting aside land in each state for agricultural colleges. Mass. Aggie, as it was called, opened in Amherst in 1863, with Henry F. French as president. French, however, ran the college without students until 1867 when, after much red tape, the buildings were ready.

THE DURFEE PLANT HOUSE, MASSACHUSETTS AGRICULTURAL COLLEGE, 1878. When the first class of thirty-three students, led by four professors, began in 1867, a feature of the new campus was the botanical plant house. Dr. Nathan Durfee, along with Leonard and Henry Hills, donated the funds. The year 1867 also marked the start of the tenure of William S. Clark as president. Clark did great things for the college, and also founded Hokkaido University in Japan, where his advice, "Boys, be ambitious!" is still quoted today.

MASSACHUSETTS AGRICULTURAL COLLEGE, FROM THE DURFEE PLANT HOUSE, AFTER 1886. Levi Stockbridge and Henry Goodell followed Clark as presidents. By 1905, there were about 250 students. The college's Stone Chapel was added in 1886, but the campus didn't yet have the pond that is central to it today.

MASSACHUSETTS AGRICULTURAL COLLEGE ROPE PULL, c. 1915. After the College Pond was built, the students made quick use of it as the site for rope pulling competitions between lower and upper classes. The winning class won the rope, which they cut into one-foot lengths and hung in their rooms as trophies.

SCORING CHICKENS AT MASSACHUSETTS
AGRICULTURAL COLLEGE, 1910. Mr.
Lambert scores the finer points of a
chicken in a poultry course. Female
students, seen in this photograph, began
to be admitted in 1892, and by 1931,
when the name changed to
Massachusetts State College, women
comprised 216 of 760 students. In 1947,
the college became the University of
Massachusetts.

HAMPSHIRE COLLEGE, THE JOHNSON
LIBRARY CENTER. In 1970, a small,
highly innovative college was started in
South Amherst, on and around Tinker
Hill, with the academic support of
Amherst College, Smith, Mount
Holyoke, and the University of
Massachusetts. The Five Colleges, as
they began to be known, would share
ideas and programs, with Hampshire
acting almost as an experimental
laboratory.

THE ELECTRONIC MUSIC STUDIO AT HAMPSHIRE COLLEGE, 1970s. Hampshire was one of the first colleges to use the groundbreaking Moog synthesizer in music studies.

HAMPSHIRE COLLEGE STUDENTS. When Hampshire held its Inaugural Convocation in 1970, the great historian Henry Steele Commager was awarded an honorary Doctor of Letters Degree. At the opening ceremonies the students honored a popular professor with their own Doctor of the Occult Degree and gave him a psychedelic sequined academic robe.

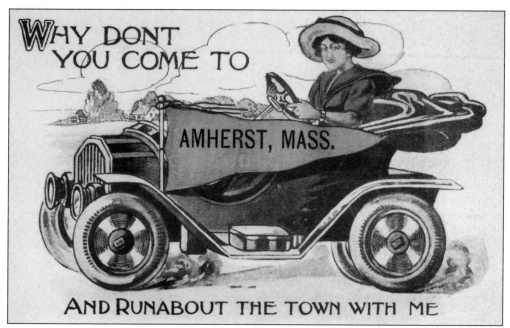

TOURIST POSTCARDS. When auto-touring became popular, Amherst issued postcards like the ones on this and the following page. Oddly enough, the Dutch images bear no relationship to the town.

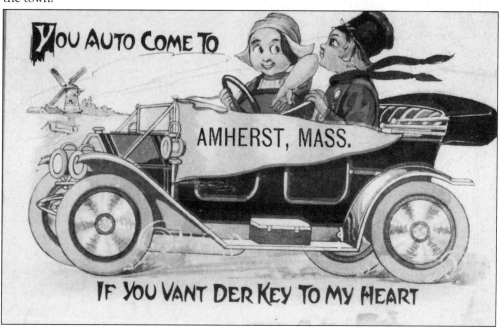

Nine

Hadley:

The River's Flood, the Fugitives' Retreat,
and a Classic Mountain Resort

THE HADLEY COMMON, WEST STREET, *c.* 1905. Reverend John Russell led his congregation from Wethersfield, Connecticut, to this site where they founded Hadley in 1659. On land known by Native Americans as Norwottuck Meadow, a broad Common was laid out in a large bend of the Connecticut River, with the river bordering each end.

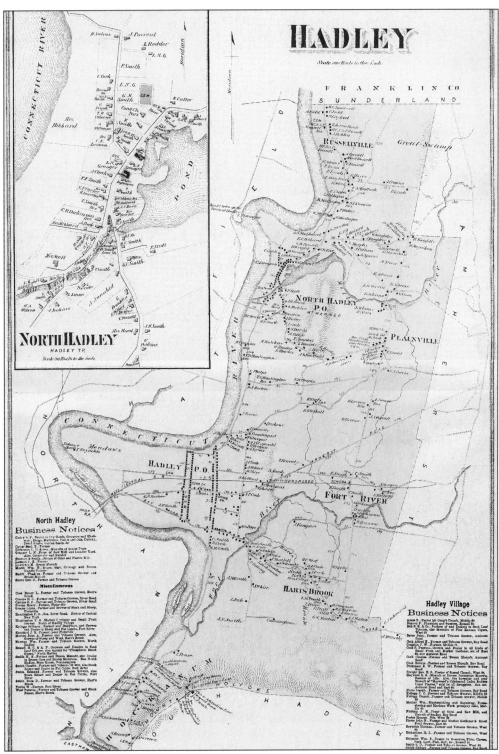

A Map of Hadley, from the County Atlas of Hampshire Massachusetts (F.W. Beers, New York, 1873).

98

THE CONGREGATIONAL CHURCH, MIDDLE STREET. In 1663, the first of three churches was built on the West Street Common. In 1683, the congregation became obsessed with witches, and accused Mary Webster of "having familiarity with the devil." She was hung and then buried in the snow. The fact that she survived was taken as proof she was a witch. The above church was built in 1841, when, to the dismay of those on West Street, the congregation moved to Middle Street.

RUSSELL CHURCH, HADLEY COMMON. Residents around the West Street Common were sufficiently put out by the moving of the Congregational Church to Middle Street, that they built the Russell Church in 1841. Unable to support two Congregational churches so close together, the Russell Church was moved in about 1913 to Russell Street. There it served as Holy Rosary Catholic Church until it was torn down in 1983.

OLD HADLEY COMMON, WOODCUT, 1850s. The building in the center was the site of Reverend John Russell's house, where the Regicides were hidden. William Goffe and Edward Whalley had condemned Charles I to death and, in 1660, had to leave England when Charles II ascended the throne. In 1664, the fugitives found sanctuary in Reverend Russell's house in Hadley. While agents of the king scoured New England, the Regicides hid for at least twelve years in Hadley.

THE PERILS OF OUR FOREFATHERS BY FREDERICK CHAPMAN. The legend goes that in September of 1675, while the townspeople were at church, fugitive William Goffe saw Indians approaching from his hideout. In order to save the town, Goffe revealed himself by rushing into church, white beard flowing, to save the town from attack. He supposedly led the town in fending off the assault, then disappeared. Goffe has since been known as "The Angel of Hadley."

TOWN HALL AND THE CONGREGATIONAL CHURCH, MIDDLE STREET, c. 1910. Children play along Middle Street before Dutch Elm disease and the Hurricane of 1938 destroyed the elegant elms. By this time, parts of the vast expanse of Old Hadley had been divided into Hatfield, Sunderland, South Hadley, Amherst, and Granby.

HADLEY BLACKSMITH BILL MATHERS. Carriages, pungs, sleighs, wagons, plows, and the horses and oxen that pulled them, were all cared for and shod by blacksmiths like Bill Mathers.

MATHER'S BLACKSMITH SHOP, CORNER OF MIDDLE STREET AND BAY ROAD. Blacksmiths Mather and Rice shod many sleighs, on which rides "were pleasant in cold nights," according to historian Sylvester Judd, "when the moon shone brightly, and the snow was of dazzling whiteness, and the bells jingled and the runners creaked and hissed. There were no buffalo robes, but plenty of warm blankets. Now and then a load of young people were overturned into the snow, but this usually occasioned more mirth than injury."

THE BEN SMITH TAVERN, BAY ROAD, 1909. Ethan Allen, owner of this seventeen-room house early in this century, posed at the bar. This popular tavern and ballroom, built by Major John Smith in 1774, was on Bay Road, a major route between Boston and Albany. When a Catholic priest was sent to Northampton in 1806 to attend the condemned men, it is said Protestant Northampton refused him, and he stayed instead at Smith's Tavern.

THE SAMUEL PORTER HOUSE, WEST STREET, EARLY 1900s. Samuel Porter Jr. built this house in 1713, and today it's the oldest standing structure in Hadley. Porter is said to be the first white child born in town. He was a trader, judge, and sheriff. During the flood of 1936, saddle horses were kept in the room where early court sessions were held, and supplies were brought through the door by canoe.

THE PORTER-PHELPS-HUNTINGTON HOUSE, FROM THE GREAT BARN DOOR, RIVER DRIVE. Moses Porter built the first house outside the palisade of Hadley in 1752, and was killed in the French and Indian Wars. The house was enlarged by Charles Phelps, but has remained structurally unchanged since 1799. Frederic Dan Huntington, bishop of central New York, spent summers here until 1904. Open to the public, the rooms and furnishings remain as they were for generations.

THE DOORWAY OF THE SAMUEL PORTER
HOUSE, WEST STREET. Emma
McQueston stands in the doorway of
the 1713 house. This doorway, with its
raised pilasters, scrolled pediment, and
double-leaf doors, is an elegant example
of a classic eighteenth-century
Connecticut Valley doorway.

THE HADLEY FARM MUSEUM, RUSSELL
STREET, c. 1930. Bookstore owner
Henry R. Johnson and photographer
and writer Clifton Johnson started a
museum for the farm implements Henry
had collected. A 1782 barn at the
Porter-Phelps-Huntington House was
about to be torn down, so the brothers
had it moved to the center of town. It
opened in 1930, housing myriad bits of
agricultural history reflecting the town's
broom-making and asparagus-growing
past.

HARD TIMES FOR MARY AND LEVI ADAMS. Hadley wagon maker Levi Adams and his wife Mary had six children when medicine and psychology were little understood. Emma was born in 1850. After her one-and-one-half-year-old sister Sarah died, and her brother William drowned before his 4th birthday, her health declined. Her friends feared for her sanity but could do nothing. She took her own life in 1878, and a newspaper commented, "Poor girl, she sleeps at last—the sleep that knows no waking."

HOPKINS ACADEMY, RUSSELL STREET, *c.* 1910. Hopkins Academy, founded in 1664, was one of the earliest secondary schools in the area. Students came from great distances to attend, and by 1837 there were three hundred from all over the Commonwealth. The building shown here, formerly Dr. Franklin Bonney's residence, housed the Academy from 1909 to 1954.

SHIPMAN'S GROCERIES, RUSSELL STREET, *c.* 1900. Here, one could tie a horse to the hitching posts out front, shop for groceries, pick up the mail, make a telephone call, or have some of "W.W. Boynton's Ice Cold Soda."

THE GENERAL JOSEPH HOOKER HOUSE, WEST STREET, 1890s. Joseph Hooker was born here in 1814. After graduating from Hopkins Academy and West Point, President Abraham Lincoln appointed him to command the Union Army of the Potomac 1863. This house burned down in 1898.

OCTOBER HARVEST IN FORT MEADOW. In the 1890s, the young were drawn away from farms, causing a labor shortage and a drop in land values. Chauncey Parson recruited twenty Polish men from the docks of New York, and soon more immigrated. They prospered and eventually bought their own farms. At first, local papers declared the Polish dangerous. In 1927, however, the same papers declared that "the Polish farmer has saved the Valley . . . They possess a vigor, an unending patience that has somehow been lost by the New Englander."

Ten

North Hadley:
Tobacco, Broom Corn, and Potatoes

THE NORTH HADLEY MILL POND. By the end of the seventeenth century, the Mill River attracted millers and farmers to the north end of town. Few families lived there until the early nineteenth century, when a summer Sabbath School was set up for the children of grist and saw millers, blacksmiths, and farmers. The Sabbath School met in the schoolhouse, and after a religious society was begun 1831, professors from Amherst College preached there.

THE SECOND CONGREGATIONAL CHURCH, NORTH HADLEY. Having outgrown the schoolhouse as a place of worship, and needing a church closer than the one at Hadley Common, North Hadley built its own church in 1834. Today it is particularly known for its fine Johnson pipe organ, installed in 1866.

THE DICKINSON BROOM TOOL MILL, MILL RIVER. After buying water rights on the Mill River in 1840, Caleb D. Dickinson became a major New England broom-tool maker. His son-in-law, John C. Howe, joined the business in 1870, and the factory continued to make broom tools and knives until the mid-1960s. A significant crop in Hadley was broom corn, with which dozens of local shops made brooms—using Caleb Dickinson's tools.

NORTH HADLEY CENTER, EARLY 1900s. The general store on the left sold "Jap-a-Lag" wood stain (advertised on the end wall), contained the North Hadley Post Office, and had an early public telephone. Grains from surrounding towns were brought to the gristmill (right) to be ground into flour.

A NORTH HADLEY FARM, EARLY 1900s. This farm beside the Connecticut River, like most, was prone to floods every spring, which caused great damage, but also deposited rich silt in the fields. To the left is Indian Hill, a Native American burial ground; Mt. Warner is in the distance.

A North Hadley Farmer, early 1900s. This unknown farmer standing in his stable door may have grown tobacco, broom corn, or potatoes. In any case, his farm was on some of the best agricultural land in the Northeast, land quickly being lost.

Eleven

The Connecticut River:
"A Perfect Stream for a Poet"
—Washington Irving

THE CONNECTICUT RIVER, FROM MOUNT HOLYOKE. Hadley photographer and writer Clifton Johnson photographed his children—Robert, Margaret, and Arthur—on Mt. Holyoke in about 1910. The first traveler to describe this view was Reverend Paul Coffin of Maine who, in 1760, wrote in his diary, "The View here far exceeds all I ever had before. Hundreds of Acres of Wheat, Rye, Peas, Flax, Oats, Corn, &c., look like a beautiful garden, variously yet elegantly laid out."

LOGS ON THE CONNECTICUT RIVER, 1908. The river, the longest in New England, was the principle avenue of transportation before railroads. Logs, onions, tobacco, textiles, clocks, and guns were carried downriver to markets elsewhere. Upriver came cotton from the South, silk from the Orient, and sugar and rum from the West Indies.

MARGARET JOHNSON AND "GRANDPA" LYMAN FISHING ON THE RIVER, c. 1906. In the nineteenth century, the river held abundant fish. The *American Gazetteer* of 1810 reported, "Sturgeon, salmon, and shad, are caught in plenty in their season, from the mouth of the river upwards."

ICE CUTTING ON A COVE OF THE CONNECTICUT RIVER, c. 1905. Many rural families cut their own ice from ponds, coves, and streams, and stored it in ice houses that were sometimes dug into the ground. Blocks of ice cooled kitchen ice boxes made of wood and lined with tin or zinc.

SPRING FLOOD ON THE CONNECTICUT, 1901. Hadley farmers grew accustomed to annual floods of the river. Heavy flooding in 1854, 1862, 1866, 1909, and 1913, resulted in unusual destruction. However, the Flood of 1936 and the Hurricane of 1938 were unparalleled disasters, with many lives and farms lost.

THE HOCKANUM FERRY, c. 1905. By 1658, the Hockanum Ferry was carrying people, carriages, wagons, and animals between Hadley and Northampton. The first bridge was built in 1808, making passage by stage coach possible. A covered bridge replaced it in 1826, when it was washed away by a flood. In 1877, a tornado destroyed the covered bridge, sending six teams of horses into the river, killing Catharine Sullivan and sending little Fred Cook into a tree, unharmed.

THE HADLEY TROLLEY BRIDGE, c. 1905. By the turn-of-the-century, three bridges cluttered the river between Hadley and Northampton: a trolley bridge, one for wagons and carriages, and one for railroad trains. Two were replaced by the Coolidge Bridge in 1939. Today, the railroad bridge serves bicyclists and rollerbladers on the Norwottuck Rail Trail.

Twelve
Hockanum:
The Meadow below the Mountain

HAYING IN THE HOCKANUM MEADOWS, 1890s. Hockanum, in the south end of Hadley, is strikingly beautiful. Bordered on the northwest by the Connecticut River, its meadows bump abruptly against dramatic Mount Holyoke on the southeast.

Mowing Hay in Hockanum, 1890s. Though Hockanum was an Indian name, it was actually given to this area by the English, who had encountered the name in East Hartford, Connecticut. These pleasant meadows attracted Calvin Coolidge while he studied law in Northampton. Having been brought up in Vermont, he missed the country and occasionally rode a horse rake in Hockanum.

THE HOCKANUM COVERED BRIDGE, EARLY 1900s. This bridge crossed the Fort River at the north end of Hockanum. The river cuts through South Amherst and Hadley before emptying into the Connecticut River. It was named for the Norwottuck Indian fort that stood above the steep banks of the river, about 300 yards east of the Connecticut River.

FLOODING OF THE CONNECTICUT RIVER, 1927. The perpetual flooding of the river could result in disaster, or exotic boat rides, depending on one's perspective.

THE HOCKANUM SCHOOL, c. 1930. This rural town required several schools to reach its scattered population. Besides the Hockanum School there were primary schools on West Street, Middle Street, Bay Road, in North Hadley, and in the Russellville and Plainville sections of town.

THE HOCKANUM SCHOOL CLASSROOM, EARLY 1900s. Students warm themselves around the wood stove while eating lunch.

CLIFTON JOHNSON AND SON ROGER, AT APPLE PICKING TIME, 1910. Hockanum native Clifton Johnson was a remarkable photographer, biographer, and travel writer. In thousands of photographs and over one hundred books, he documented the early twentieth-century lives of ordinary people in nearly every state and many European countries. Many of his extraordinary photographs illustrate the Hadley chapters of this book.

A PORTRAIT BY CLIFTON JOHNSON. "Grandpa" Loren Pease was photographed many times on his rambling Hockanum farm by Clifton Johnson.

IRVING JOHNSON HUSKING CORN, 1920. Clifton's son Irving, born in 1905, grew up to be one of the most famous twentieth-century men of the sea. He and his wife Electa sailed around the world eight times in the *Yankee*. Their adventures in such places as Tahiti, the Galapagos Islands, the New Hebrides, and on Easter Island, resulted in eight books, National Geographic Magazine articles, and films.

MARGARET JOHNSON, 1899. Clifton Johnson had a gift for photographing people—especially children. His daughter Margaret was a frequent subject on the family farm.

Thirteen
Mount Holyoke:
"A Beautiful Picture Seldom Rivaled"
—Ralph Waldo Emerson

VIEW FROM MOUNT HOLYOKE, ENGRAVING BY WILLIAM H. BARTLETT, 1836–37. One of New England's most fashionable and flourishing summer resorts was on top of Mount Holyoke. The beauty of the spot was recognized early. In 1823, Ralph Waldo Emerson wrote, "The prospect repays the ascent . . . the broad meadows in the immediate vicinity of the mountain through which the Connecticut winds made a beautiful picture seldom rivaled."

SUMMIT HOUSE, MOUNT HOLYOKE, c. 1870. The first house raised on the summit was thrown up in one day in 1821. In 1849, John Watton French of Northampton bought the structure, which had gone through several changes, and 10 acres. When he completed his "Prospect House" in 1851, he invited the international singing star Jenny Lind to appear at the dedication ceremonies.

MOUNT HOLYOKE, MASS.

AN ADVERTISING CARD, MOUNT HOLYOKE, 1860s. The view from the mountain achieved great fame—Thomas Cole's painting *The Oxbow* hangs in the Metropolitan Museum of Art, New York. With the increasing number of visitors, the first tramway was built from the river to Prospect House in 1854.

AN ADVERTISING BROADSIDE, 1879. John French continually added rooms to the resort, and in 1867 he built a larger, double-track tramway to the top. A steamboat was purchased to pick up passengers at the Mount Tom and Holyoke railroad stations. Eventually the list of visitors included Alexander Graham Bell, Henry Wadsworth Longfellow, and Presidents McKinley, Coolidge, and Taft.

Mt. HOLYOKE.

The Finest View in New England.

Telegraph and Telephone Connections at Prospect House on Summit.

P. O. ADDRESS,	J. W. FRENCH,
Mount Holyoke,	South Hadley, Mass.

Named in 1654 after Capt. ELIZUR HOLYOKE.
Perpendicular Elevation 1000 Feet.

Has been visited longer than any other Mountain in New England ; "Men climbed the Mountain to view the country in 1676."
Judd's History of Hadley.

"In the View from Mt. Holyoke the grand and beautiful are united."
Mass. State Geology.

"Mt. Holyoke is the gem of Massachusetts Mountains, and the one more visited than all others."
Hitchcock, in Holland's History of West. Mass.

The first Railway was built in 1854 ; the present track in 1867.

More than half a million visitors have been over it. People of all ages visit it. A lady rode up a few years ago who visited the Mountain 79 years before. We see people every year who visited the Mountain 30, 40, 50 and 60 years before.

Mt. Holyoke is in Hampshire Co., Mass.

117	Miles	from	BOSTON,	by Railroad
153	"	"	NEW YORK,	"
79	"	"	NEW HAVEN,	"
43	"	"	HARTFORD,	"
118	"	"	ALBANY,	"

FROM THE
"PROSPECT HOUSE,"

Can be seen Mountains in four States, also forty towns—thirty-two in Mass., and eight in Conn., viz:

MOUNTAINS.

Monadnock, N. H.; Green, Vt.; East and West Rock, New Haven, Conn.; Talcott, Avon, Conn.; Greylock, Mass.; Wachusett, Mass.; Sugar Loaf, Mass.; Norwottock, Mass.; Toby, Mass.; Tom, Mass.; Nonatuck, Mass.

TOWNS.

Northampton, Haydenville, Williamsburg, Goshen, Hadley, Hatfield, Whateley, South Deerfield, Greenfield, Shelburne, Sunderland, North Hadley, North Amherst, Amherst, South Amherst, Pelham, Belchertown, Granby, Ludlow, South Hadley, Wilbraham, North Wilbraham, Springfield, Chicopee, Holyoke, Longmeadow, West Springfield, Agawam, South Hampton, Easthampton, Montgomery, Blandford, Mass. Thompsonville, Windsor, East Windsor, Enfield, Hartford, West Hartford, Suffield and Somers, Conn.

OBJECTS OF INTEREST.

State Lunatic Hospital, Round Hill, Clark Institute for the Deaf and Dumb, and Smith Female College, at Northampton; Williston Seminary, at East Hampton; Amherst College, Agricultural College and Mount Pleasant, at Amherst; Mt. Holyoke Female Seminary, at South Hadley; Wesleyan Academy, at Wilbraham; United States Armory, at Springfield; Manufacturing city of Holyoke; Old Hadley and her beautiful streets; Ox-Bow Island, Shepherd's Island, in the Connecticut River.

Railway from stable to summit, 600 feet; number of steps in staircase, 522 ; to, top of observatory, 568 ; perpendicular ascent from stable, 365 feet ; first house built in 1821 ; second house built in 1851 ; enlarged to present size in 1861 ; first railway in 1854 ; present track laid in 1867 ; number of passengers over the track, more than half a million.

A MOUNT HOLYOKE POSTCARD, 1910. In the 1890s, another sixty rooms were added to the hotel, but this proved to be financially unwise. In 1916 the property and 225 acres were sold to Joseph Allen Skinner, who modernized the place in the 1920s. Unfortunately, the Hurricane of 1938 caused so much damage Skinner could not restore the hotel. He offered the entire property to the state as a gift, and in 1940, it was dedicated as the Joseph Skinner State Park.